JUST BE A KID
INSPIRATIONAL COLORING BOOK

Dedication

This book is dedicated to my Mommy, Nanna, Tee Tee Ailisha,
and Tee Tee Aimee. We miss you Nanna very much.
Thank you Mommy for helping my dreams come true.

Follow Harmoni on Intagram at Star Harmoni or on Facebook at
Star Harmoni.

By Harmoni M. Cunningham

Illustrated by Monica R. Coleman, CMR Design Group, LLC

www.cmrdgllc.com, mcoleman@cmrdgllc.com, Phone: 314-609-0154

Dear kids around the world. Don't worry about what people say about you.

Just be a kid. If you are having a hard time learn to believe in yourself.

3

4

When I was six
I was worrying
a lot and not
being a kid.

My Mommy told me life is about having fun and making memories.

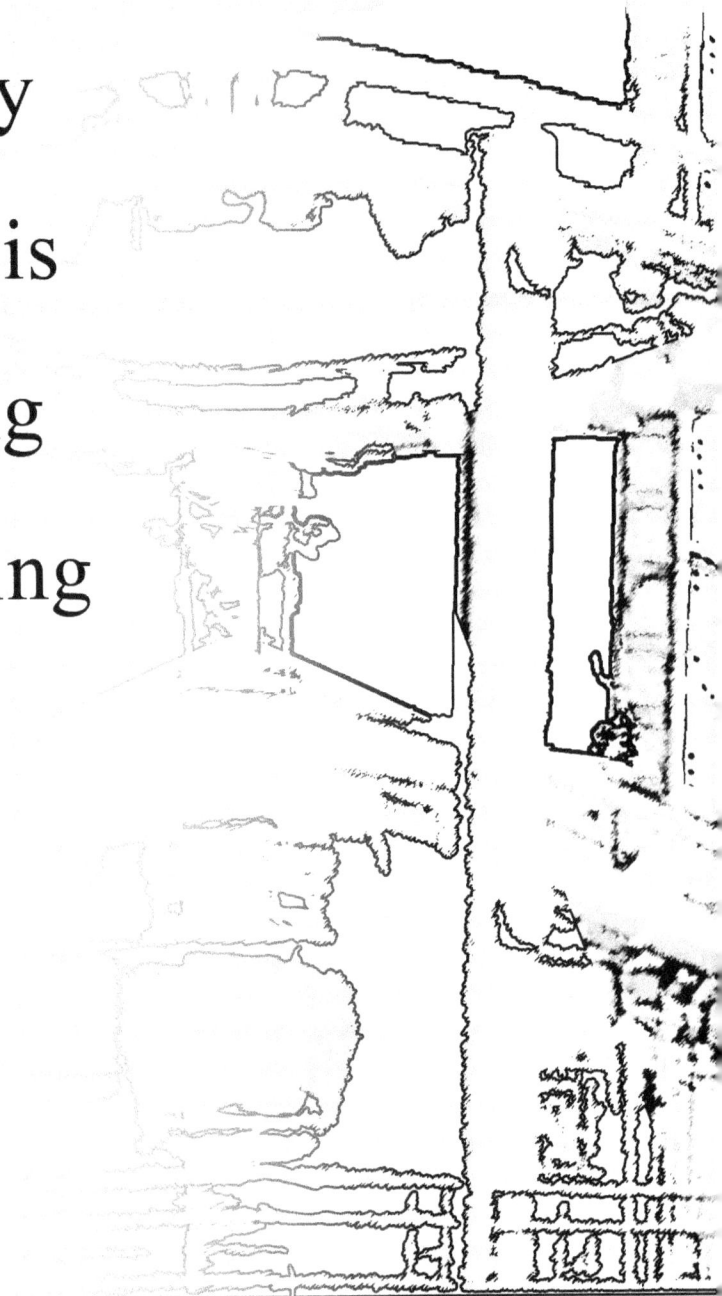

8

She told me not
to worry about
the small stuff.
Just be a kid.

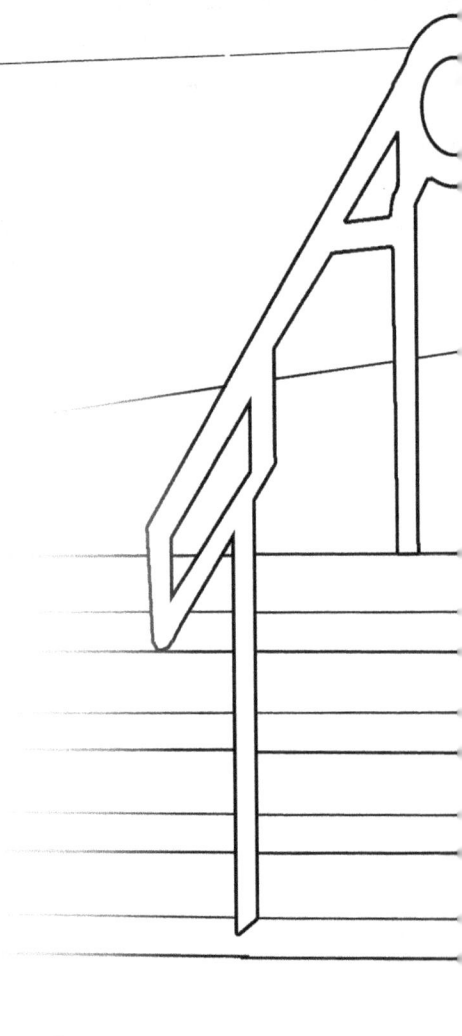

She encouraged
me, so I want to
encourage you
to just live and
love being a
kid.

Remember you can be anything you want to be. Just be a kid

Here are 5 steps on how to be a kid.

Step 1:
Keep God First

Step 2:
Don't Worry

Step 3:
Have Fun

Step 4:
Enjoy School

Step 5:
Make Friends

If you follow these five steps I'm sure you will do great in life!!

www.ingramcontent.com/pod-product-compliance
Lightning Source LLC
Chambersburg PA
CBHW081641040426
42449CB00014B/3405